Cross Stitch
FOR THE HOME

Dorothea Hall

☐MARK
PUBLISHING
5400 SCOTTS VALLEY DR.
SCOTTS VALLEY, CA 95066

Published 1992 by Merehurst Limited
Ferry House, 51-57 Lacy Road, Putney, London SW15 1PR
© Copyright 1992 Merehurst Limited

ISBN 0-937769-29-0

Distributed in the United States by
Mark Publishing, Inc.
5400 Scotts Valley Drive, Scotts Valley, CA 95066

Edited by Diana Brinton
Designed by Maggie Aldred
Photography by Di Lewis
Illustrations by John Hutchinson
Typesetting by BMD Graphics, Hemel Hempstead
Colour separation by Fotographics Limited, UK – Hong Kong
Printed in Hong Kong by Wing King Tong

*Merehurst is the leading publisher of craft books and has an excellent range
of titles to suit all levels. Please send to the address above for our
free catalogue, stating the title of this book.*

SUPPLIERS

The following mail order company has supplied some of the basic items needed for making up the projects in this book:

Framecraft Miniatures Limited
148-150 High Street
Aston
Birmingham, B6 4US
England
Telephone (021) 359 4442

Addresses for Framecraft worldwide
Ireland Needlecraft Pty. Ltd.
2-4 Keppel Drive
Hallam, Victoria 3803
Australia

Danish Art Needlework
PO Box 442, Lethbridge
Alberta T1J 3Z1
Canada

Sanyei Imports
PO Box 5, Hashima Shi
Gifu 501-62
Japan

The Embroidery Shop
286 Queen Street
Masterton
New Zealand

Anne Brinkley Designs Inc.
246 Walnut Street
Newton
Mass. 02160
USA

S A Threads and Cottons Ltd.
43 Somerset Road
Cape Town
South Africa

For information on your nearest stockist of embroidery cotton, contact the following:

DMC

USA
The DMC Corporation
Port Kearney Bld.
10 South Kearney
N.J. 07032-0650
Telephone: 201 589 0606

COATS AND ANCHOR

USA
Coats & Clark
P.O. Box 27067
Dept CO1
Greenville
SC 29616
Telephone: 803 234 0103

MADEIRA

U.S.A.
Madeira Marketing Limited
600 East 9th Street
Michigan City
IN 46360
Telephone: 219 873 1000

CONTENTS

INTRODUCTION

The immense popularity of cross stitch embroidery, with its distinctive range of decorative effects, can be seen in the growing interest for hand-embroidered items for the home. The collection in this book includes a traditional sampler based on the house and garden theme, a footstool in the Victorian style, showing a 'Lion and the Unicorn' design, and many pretty placemats and pictures.

Cross stitch is a wonderfully easy stitch to learn and you do not require years of experience to produce very pleasing results. Each design is carefully charted and colour coded and has accompanying step-by-step instructions for making up the item.

While some designs are very easy and quite suitable for beginners, others are a little more challenging and may involve working with many colours. Handling them can seem daunting at first, but your skill will very quickly improve with practice.

Leaning to work with several needles threaded with different colours is useful, and you will avoid having to start and finish new threads with each colour area.

There is also a Basic Skills section, which covers everything from preparing and stretching your fabric in an embroidery frame to mounting your cross stitch ready for display.

All the necessary skills are simply explained, thus ensuring that, whatever your experience, you will be able to enjoy creating beautiful things for every room in your home.

BASIC SKILLS

BEFORE YOU BEGIN

PREPARING THE FABRIC
Even with an average amount of handling, many evenweave fabrics tend to fray at the edges, so it is a good idea to overcast the raw edges, using ordinary sewing thread, before you begin.

THE INSTRUCTIONS
Each project begins with a full list of the materials that you will require; Aida, Tula, Lugana and Linda are all fabrics produced by Zweigart. Note that the measurements given for the embroidery fabric include a minimum of 3cm (1¼in) all around to allow for stretching it in a frame and preparing the edges to prevent them from fraying.

A colour key for DMC stranded embroidery cotton is given with each chart. It is assumed that you will need to buy one skein of each colour mentioned, even though you may use less, but where two or more skeins are needed, this information is included in the main list of requirements.

Should you wish to use Coats/Anchor, or Madeira, stranded embroidery cottons, refer to the conversion chart given at the back of the book (page 48).

To work from the charts, particularly those where several symbols are used in close proximity, some readers may find it helpful to have the chart enlarged so that the squares and symbols can be seen more easily. Many photocopying services will do this for a minimum charge.

Before you begin to embroider, always mark the centre of the design with two lines of basting stitches, one vertical and one horizontal, running from edge to edge of the fabric, as indicated by the arrows on the charts.

As you stitch, use the centre lines given on the chart and the basting threads on your fabric as reference points for counting the squares and threads to position your design accurately.

WORKING IN A HOOP
A hoop is the most popular frame for use with small areas of embroidery. It consists of two rings, one fitted inside the other; the outer ring usually has an

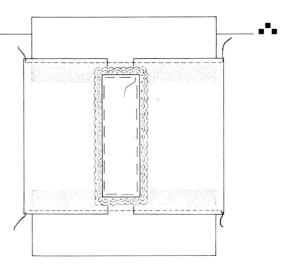

adjustable screw attachment so that it can be tightened to hold the stretched fabric in place. Hoops are available in several sizes, ranging from 10cm (4in) in diameter to quilting hoops with a diameter of 38cm (15in). Hoops with table stands or floor stands attached are also available.

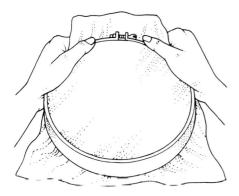

1 To stretch your fabric in a hoop, place the area to be embroidered over the inner ring and press the outer ring over it with the tension screw released. Tissue paper can be placed between the outer ring and the embroidery, so that the hoop does not mark the fabric. Lay the tissue paper over the fabric when you set it in the hoop, then tear away the central, embroidery area.

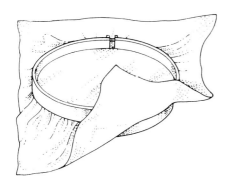

2 Smooth the fabric and, if needed, straighten the grain before tightening the screw. The fabric should be evenly stretched.

EXTENDING EMBROIDERY FABRIC

It is easy to extend a piece of embroidery fabric, such as a bookmark, to stretch it in a hoop.

● Fabric oddments of a similar weight can be used. Simply cut four pieces to size (in other words, to the measurement that will fit both the embroidery fabric and your hoop) and baste them to each side

of the embroidery fabric before stretching it in the hoop in the usual way.

WORKING IN A RECTANGULAR FRAME

Rectangular frames are more suitable for larger pieces of embroidery. They consist of two rollers, with tapes attached, and two flat side pieces, which slot into the rollers and are held in place by pegs or screw attachments. Available in different sizes, either alone or with adjustable table or floor stands, frames are measured by the length of the roller tape, and range in size from 30cm (12in) to 68cm (27in).

As alternatives to a slate frame, canvas stretchers and the backs of old picture frames can be used. Provided there is sufficient extra fabric around the finished size of the embroidery, the edges can be turned under and simply attached with drawing pins (thumb tacks) or staples.

1 To stretch your fabric in a rectangular frame, cut out the fabric, allowing at least an extra 5cm (2in) all around the finished size of the embroidery. Baste a single 12mm (½in) turning on the top and bottom edges and oversew strong tape, 2.5cm (1in) wide, to the other two sides. Mark the centre line both ways with basting stitches. Working from the centre outwards and using strong thread, oversew the top and bottom edges to the roller tapes. Fit the side pieces into the slots, and roll any extra fabric on one roller until the fabric is taut.

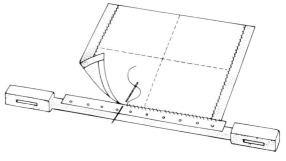

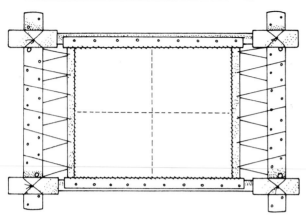

2 Insert the pegs or adjust the screw attachments to secure the frame. Thread a large-eyed needle (chenille needle) with strong thread or fine string and lace both edges, securing the ends around the intersections of the frame. Lace the webbing at 2.5cm (1in) intervals, stretching the fabric evenly.

ENLARGING A GRAPH PATTERN

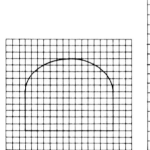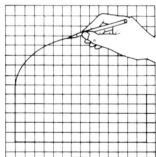

● To enlarge a graph pattern, you will need a sheet of graph paper ruled in 1cm (⅜in) squares, a ruler and pencil. If, for example, the scale is one square to 5cm (2in) you should first mark the appropriate lines to give a grid of the correct size. Copy the graph freehand from the small grid to the larger one, completing one square at a time. Use a ruler to draw the straight lines first, and then copy the freehand curves.

TO BIND AN EDGE

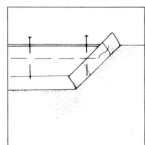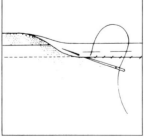

1 Open out the turning on one edge of the bias binding and pin in position on the right side of the fabric, matching the fold to the seamline. Fold over the cut end of the binding. Finish by overlapping the starting point by about 12mm (½in). Baste and machine stitch along the seamline.

2 Fold the binding over the raw edge to the wrong side, baste and, using matching sewing thread, neatly hem to finish.

PIPED SEAMS

Contrasting piping adds a special decorative finish to a seam and looks particularly attractive on items such as cushions and cosies.

You can cover piping cord with either bias-cut fabric of your choice or a bias binding; alternatively, ready-covered piping cord is available in several widths and many colours.

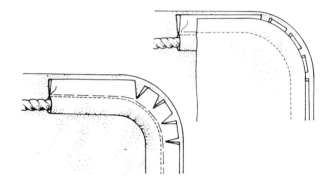

1 To apply piping, pin and baste it to the right side of the fabric, with seam lines matching. Clip into the seam allowance where necessary.

2 With right sides together, place the second piece of fabric on top, enclosing the piping. Baste and then either hand stitch in place or machine stitch, using a zipper foot. Stitch as close to the piping as possible, covering the first line of stitching.

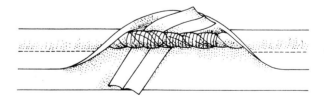

3 To join ends of piping cord together, first overlap the two ends by about 2.5cm (1in). Unpick the two cut ends of bias to reveal the cord. Join the bias strip as shown. Trim and press the seam open. Unravel and splice the two ends of the cord. Fold the bias strip over it, and finish basting around the edge.

MOUNTING EMBROIDERY

The cardboard should be cut to the size of the finished embroidery, with an extra 6mm (¼in) added all around to allow for the recess in the frame.

LIGHTWEIGHT FABRICS

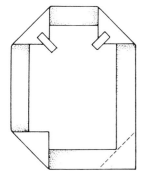 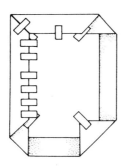

1 Place the emboidery face down, with the cardboard centred on top, and basting and pencil lines matching. Begin by folding over the fabric at each corner and securing it with masking tape.

2 Working first on one side and then the other, fold over the fabric on all sides and secure it firmly with pieces of masking tape, placed about 2.5cm (1in) apart. Also neaten the mitred corners with masking tape, pulling the fabric tightly to give a firm, smooth finish.

HEAVIER FABRICS

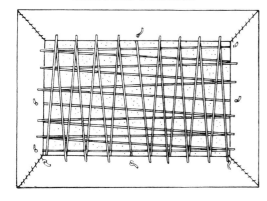

● Lay the embroidery face down, with the cardboard centred on top; fold over the edges of the fabric on opposite sides, making mitred folds at the corners, and lace across, using strong thread. Repeat on the other two sides. Finally, pull up the stitches fairly tightly to stretch the fabric firmly over the cardboard. Overstitch the mitred corners.

CROSS STITCH

For all cross stitch embroidery, the following two methods of working are used. In each case, neat rows of vertical stitches are produced on the back of the fabric.

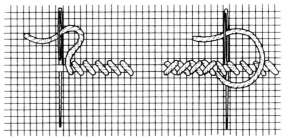

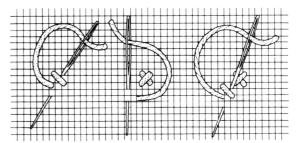

● When stitching large areas, work in horizontal rows. Working from right to left, complete the first row of evenly spaced diagonal stitches over the number of threads specified in the project instructions. Then, working from left to right, repeat the process. Continue in this way, making sure each stitch crosses in the same direction.

● When stitching diagonal lines, work downwards, completing each stitch before moving to the next.

BACKSTITCH

Backstitch is used in the projects to give emphasis to a particular foldline, an outline or a shadow. The stitches are worked over the same number of threads as the cross stitch, forming continuous straight or diagonal lines.

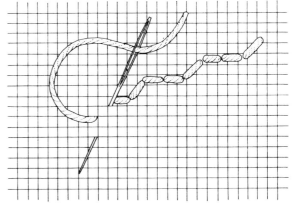

● Make the first stitch from left to right; pass the needle behind the fabric, and bring it out one stitch length ahead to the left. Repeat and continue in this way along the line.

House and Garden Sampler

Country accents abound in this sampler in the traditional style, based on the house-and-garden theme. To personalize the design, you could, with a little judicious pre-planning, depict your own house, add your initials (and the date) and, using the alphabet in the sampler design, even add a motto or dedication.

HOUSE AND GARDEN SAMPLER

YOU WILL NEED

For a Sampler measuring 23cm (9in) square
(unframed):

*35cm (14in) square of white linen, 26 threads to
2.5cm (1in)
DMC stranded embroidery cotton in the colours
given in the panel
23cm (9in) square of 3mm (⅛in) cardboard for
mounting the embroidery
23cm (9in) square of lightweight synthetic batting
Strong thread for securing the mounted fabric
Picture frame of your choice
No26 tapestry needle*

•

Following the alphabet given with the sampler,
select your chosen initials and, using a soft pencil,
draw them on the chart. For three initials, ignore the
centre diamond and experiment with the spacing,
positioning them within the central area. You may
prefer to add the date of the embroidery, or a longer
dedication. In which case, ignore the two hearts and
the two outer diamonds and use the whole of the
lower area. You will find it easier to follow if this is
charted on a separate piece of graph paper, matching
the grid to that given in the book. If you do remove
the hearts, it would be nice to work the embroidery
in red, or perhaps the blue, from the border. Which-
ever colour you use, it will be helpful to chart your
wording as a guide before working the embroidery.

THE EMBROIDERY

With the prepared fabric stretched in a frame, see
page 5, and the centre lines basted both ways,
begin the embroidery. Using two strands of thread
in the needle and carefully following the chart,
complete the embroidery, working one cross stitch
over two threads of fabric. Remember that with very
openweave fabrics it is important not to strand the
thread from one area to another, otherwise it will
show through on the right side. Begin and finish

threads underneath an embroidered area, and trim
all loose ends when finishing.

Remove the finished embroidery from the frame,
but do not take out the basting threads at this stage.
Steam press on the wrong side.

FRAMING THE SAMPLER

A thin layer of batting is placed between the cardboard and the embroidery. In this case it helps to
give an opaque quality to the openweave linen. To
centre the cardboard over the embroidery, first
mark the centre line of the cardboard both ways,
using a soft pencil. Similarly, mark the batting by
placing a pin at the central point on each side.

Lay the embroidery face down; centre the batting
on top, and then the cardboard, with basting, pins
and pencil lines matching.

Working on one side and then the opposite side,
fold over the edges of the fabric on all sides and
secure with masking tape, see page 7, first
removing the pins. Neaten the corners by folding
them in to form a mitre and secure with masking
tape. Remove the basting threads.

Insert the glass and mounted embroidery into
your picture frame; add the backing board provided, and secure with picture tacks. Cover the
tacks with broad sticky tape to neaten.

HOUSE AND GARDEN ▶			
=	ecru	✱ 351	salmon pink
◹	pale yellow		
◣ 677	naples yellow	• 350	brick red
↑ 743	soft yellow	⊐ 927	pale blue
		○ 597	blue
◆ 972	deep gold	△ 523	pale green
I 352	pale salmon pink (and bks window sashes)	⊡ 732	olive
		↓ 3012	khaki

A Child's Picture

Every picture tells a story, and this embroidery, the Little Disaster, stitched in minute detail, tells of a doting farmer and his luckless pony-ride in true pictorial style.
This elaborate picture, which uses some 26 different colours of embroidery cotton, will prove an enjoyable challenge to the more experienced cross-stitch embroiderer, and when you have finished you may well feel that it is worthy of a place in your hall or living room rather than a child's bedroom.

LITTLE DISASTER ▶

T white
⊢ 745 pale yellow
    (and bks 742*)
S 677 pale gold
    (and bks 729*)
÷ 722 orange
△ 783 ochre
⬤ 951 flesh
    (and bks 758*)
I 435 rust
    (and bks 300*)
◇ 519 blue
↑ 472 pale green
◣ 469 sap green
    (and bks 935*)
↓ 503 blue green
    (and bks 500*)
‖ 3345 dark green
✕ 712 cream
    (and bks 842*)
◣ 822 beige (bks 640)
✱ 3045 light brown
    (bks 435)
  839 dark brown
    (bks 435)
◆ 3072 pale grey
○ 926 blue grey
    (and bks 311*)
● 310 black (bks 712)
*Note: 8 additional
backstitch colours**

A CHILD'S PICTURE

YOU WILL NEED

For an unframed picture measuring
23cm (9in) square:

*35cm (14in) square of blue evenweave (Aida)
fabric, 18 threads to 2.5cm (1in)
23cm (9in) square of lightweight batting
DMC stranded embroidery cotton in the colours
given in the panel
No26 tapestry needle
23cm (9in) square of 3mm (1/8in) cardboard
Masking tape for securing the mounted fabric
Picture frame of your choice*

•

THE EMBROIDERY

Referring to the instructions on page 5, stretch
the prepared fabric in a frame. Using two strands
of thread in the needle and carefully following the
chart, begin the embroidery. Work the outline and
the two horizontal dividing lines first, making sure
you count the correct number of threads between.

Finish the cross stitching and, using a single
strand of thread, work the backstitching to complete the embroidery.

Remove the embroidery from the frame and, if
necessary, steam press on the wrong side.

FRAMING THE PICTURE

To offset the embroidery, the picture here includes
a border of background fabric 2cm (³⁄₄in) wide,
which you can easily adjust to suit your own prefer-
ence. You may wish, for example, to add a
decorative outer border of your own devising,
embroidered in cross stitching. Also, to give the
finished picture a slightly padded look, a layer of
lightweight batting is inserted between the fabric
and mounting card.

Mount the picture, following the instructions
given for the heavier fabrics on page 7, before
finally inserting it into the picture frame.

Victorian Footstool

The enduring charm of a heraldic design, in this case the fighting lion and unicorn (England versus Scotland) – adapted here to fit a traditional rosewood footstool – is sure to make this a family favourite. The central medallion is approximately 20cm (8in) across, and was designed to fit the purchased footstool, but its small scale should enable it to fit virtually any circular footstool.

VICTORIAN-STYLE FOOTSTOOL

YOU WILL NEED

For a footstool measuring 30cm (12in) across:

*46cm (18in) square of grey evenweave (Aida 718)
fabric, 14 threads to 2.5cm (1in)
DMC stranded embroidery cotton in the colours
given in the panel
No24 tapestry needle
Round footstool with wooden surround
(for suppliers, see page 2)*

•

THE EMBROIDERY

Prepare the fabric and stretch it in an embroidery frame, following the instructions given on page 5.

The cross stitching is worked with two strands of thread in the needle, with the exception of the unicorn. This is worked in three strands to emphasize the colour. Begin the cross stitching, working outwards from the middle, leaving the white unicorn until last.

Remove the finished embroidery from the frame, and if necessary, steam press it on the wrong side.

MAKING UP THE FOOTSTOOL

Follow the manufacturer's instructions for assembling the footstool, but first make a preliminary check to see if, with the top fabric (the embroidery) included, the mould fits snugly inside the outer wooden frame. If not, then it is a good idea to add a layer of synthetic batting underneath the top fabric.

Complete the assembly, but before using the footstool, coat the embroidered surface with a proprietory dust-repellant spray, as recommended by upholsterers.

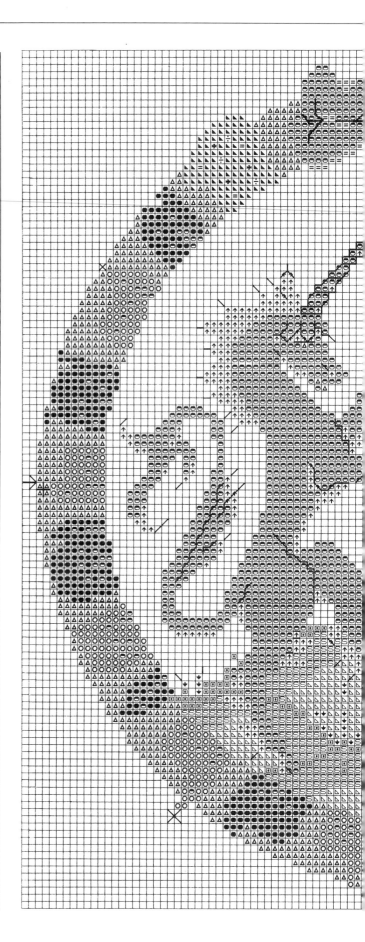

THE LION AND THE
UNICORN ◄

- ⬤ white (bks 928)
- ◣ 822 cream
- ÷ 725 yellow (bks 831)
- = 676 corn (bks on white bread)
- ○ 734 gold (bks 831)
- ◆ 831 ochre
- ● 3712 red
- △ 598 blue
- ◤ 3348 light green
- ⑀ 989 green
- ⊡ 992 veridian green
- ↓ 320 dark green
- ✳ 3045 brown (bks on brown
-      bread)
-      928 grey

Bellpull

Embroidered on white linen and
supported with wooden rods, this
miniature bellpull can be hung
as a picture.
If you have a real bell to pull,
however, it would be fun to elongate
the design, adding more leaves and
tendrills as required. To keep the
proportions, it might also be a good
idea to increase the height of the
castle turrets, windows and doors.
If the design would need to be over-
extended to reach the required length,
it would be preferable to back it with
a longer length of dark velvet.

JACK AND THE BEANSTALK ▶

↑   831 deep yellow

⊖   739 flesh (bks 3708)

✦   3708 pale pink

| 3731 pink

●   3705 bright pink

△   3772 dusky pink (bks on leaves)

⊡   315 deep dusky pink (bks 367)

✱   498 red

S   518 blue (bks 367)

✕   472 pale green (bks on trousers 611)

‖   772 peppermint green

÷   471 green

=   581 olive green

◇   3364 moss green

◣   367 dark green (bks on bird's body and legs, tendrils around tree)

✦   611 brown (bks Jack's eye)

◳   452 dove grey (bks 647; bks on diamond-shaped windows 3041*)

○   647 grey

Note: one additional backstitch colour

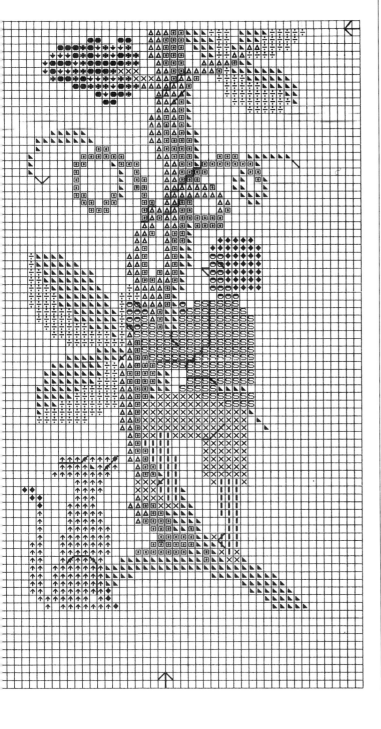

BELLPULL

YOU WILL NEED

For a bellpull measuring approximately
12cm × 43cm (4¾in × 17in):

*18cm × 56cm (7¼in × 22in) of natural-coloured
linen, 20 threads to 2.5cm (1in)
DMC stranded embroidery cotton in the colours
given in the panel
No 20 tapestry needle
60cm (24in) of white satin ribbon,
6mm (¼in) wide
Wooden rods, 13cm (5in) wide, for the bellpull
(for suppliers, see page 2)*

•

THE EMBROIDERY

Overcast the edges of the linen to prevent fraying,
and with the centre marked both ways with basting
stitches, stretch the fabric in a frame (see page
5). If you use a hoop, cover completed motifs
with tissue paper to prevent the hoop from
marking them.

Following the chart and colour keys, complete
the embroidery, using three strands of thread in
the needle throughout and making each stitch
over two threads. Steam press on the wrong
side if needed.

MAKING UP THE BELLPULL

Trim the two long edges so that the total width
across is 17cm (6¾in). Make 12mm (½in) double
turnings on these edges, basting both the top and
bottom edges of the turning to prevent the linen
from slipping – a characteristic of some linens!
Hem in place, using matching sewing thread.

On the two short edges, make a 2.5cm (1in)
turning. Make a second turning, this time 4cm
(1½in) deep, at each edge, taking the fabric over
a rod at the top and bottom. Baste and hem in
place.

Using double knots, on the inner side of the
knobs, attach the ribbon to the top rod, leaving 8cm
(3in) long ribbon tails to hang free, as shown in the
photograph.

Of Princes and Princesses

Traditional tales of adventure and of love lost and gained have been captured in this delightful set of scatter cushions, which would look charming mixed with lacy pillows.

OF PRINCES
AND PRINCESSES

YOU WILL NEED

For three cushion covers, each measuring
27.5cm (11in) square:

*35cm (14in) square each of apple green,
pink and cream evenweave Aida fabric,
14 threads to 2.5cm (1in)
30cm (12in) square each of matching or contrast
backing fabric
DMC stranded embroidery cotton in the colours
given in the appropriate panel
3 × 30cm (12in) square cushion pads
28 white seed pearls for the Swineherd design
No24 tapestry needle and No9 crewel needle
Matching sewing threads*

•

THE EMBROIDERY

All three cushions are made in the following way.
For one cushion, stretch the prepared fabric in a
frame, see page 5, and baste the centre lines in
both directions.

Using two strands of thread in the needle, and
following the appropriate chart, complete the cross
stitching. Also work the backstitching with two
strands of thread in the needle, with the exception
of the following details which are worked with a
single strand: Beauty and the Beast – the beast's
teeth and tusks; Sleeping Beauty – Beauty's face
and hands and her dress, and the prince's face. The
pearls around the Swineherd design are sewn on
with matching sewing thread and a fine crewel
needle.

Complete the embroidery by backstitching the
outline around the design, using two strands of
thread in the needle. Remove the finished embroidery from the frame and steam press on the wrong
side. Do not over press the pearls.

MAKING UP THE CUSHION

Using the basting threads as a guide, trim the edges
of the embroidery symmetrically to measure 30cm

(12in) square. Place the backing fabric and the
embroidery right sides together, baste and machine
stitch around the edges, taking a 12mm (½in)
seam, and leaving a 20cm (8in) opening in the
middle of one side.

Trim across the corners and turn the cover
through to the right side. Insert the cushion pad
and, using matching sewing thread, slipstitch the
opening to close.

Attach a small tassel to each corner of the border.
To make a tassel, wind matching embroidery thread
(six strands) five or six times around a narrow piece
of card, about 2cm (¾in) wide. Thread a needle
with a short length of thread (two strands), slip the
threads off the card and wind the thread several
times around, close to the top, making the normal
tassel shape. Pass the needle through the loops at
the top and repeat a second time. Pull the thread
firmly and bring the needle up through the centre,
ready to sew the tassel in place.

Cut through the loops at the bottom of the tassel;
fan out the threads, and trim across. Neatly stitch
a tassel to each corner, as shown in the photograph.

STITCHING ON BEADS

Use the same method to attach small, even-shaped
beads and pearls.

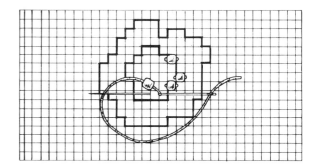

• Using either a fine crewel needle, number 9 or
10, or a beading straw for very fine beads, and
sewing thread or fine silk, bring out the needle and
thread on a bead. Reinsert the needle through the
same hole, then make a stitch the width of the bead
(and in this case, the width of the cross stitch), and
pull through, with the thread below the needle.
Repeat, completing the design as instructed.

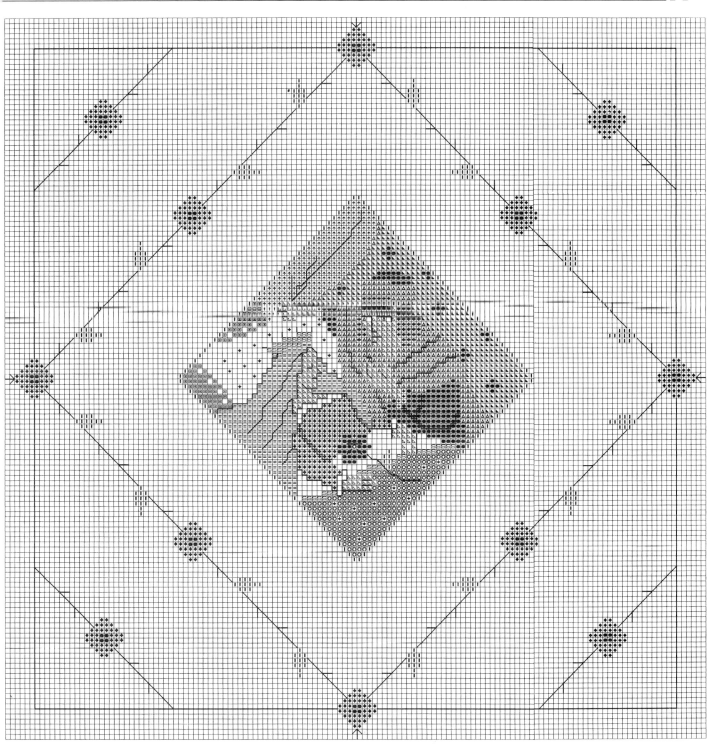

SLEEPING BEAUTY ▲

☐ white
= 3078 pale yellow (bks 743)
○ 743 yellow
⑇ 733 gold (bks on Beauty's face and hands, and outer lines on hair)
➧ gold thread
◺ 754 flesh (bks 732 for prince)
● 351 red (bks around Beauty's dress and the mouths of both figures)
◆ 747 pale blue
△ 924 dark blue (bks 504)
↑ 504 pale green
❙ 581 green (ground pattern and thorns)
✱ 732 deep olive (bks on prince's face)
◣ 644 fawn
⊡ 613 light brown

SLEEPING BEAUTY

Coming to the rescue of the stricken
parents, the last fairy announced
that although she could not
completely destroy the curse, she
could soften its effect:
'Rose will prick her finger, but she
will not die. Instead she and all
within the palace will fall asleep
until one day a prince's kiss will
wake her.'

THE SWINEHERD

In exchange for one hundred kisses
the swineherd agrees to give the
princess his pretty little pipkin,
with tinkling bells that make the
sweetest music, which has
completely won the heart of the
greedy princess.

BEAUTY AND THE BEAST

Remembering her dream, Beauty flew to the
garden where she found poor Beast stretched
out, quite senseless, as though dead. 'Beast,
oh Beast,' she wept, lifting his huge head onto
her lap. 'You must not die, I love you.'

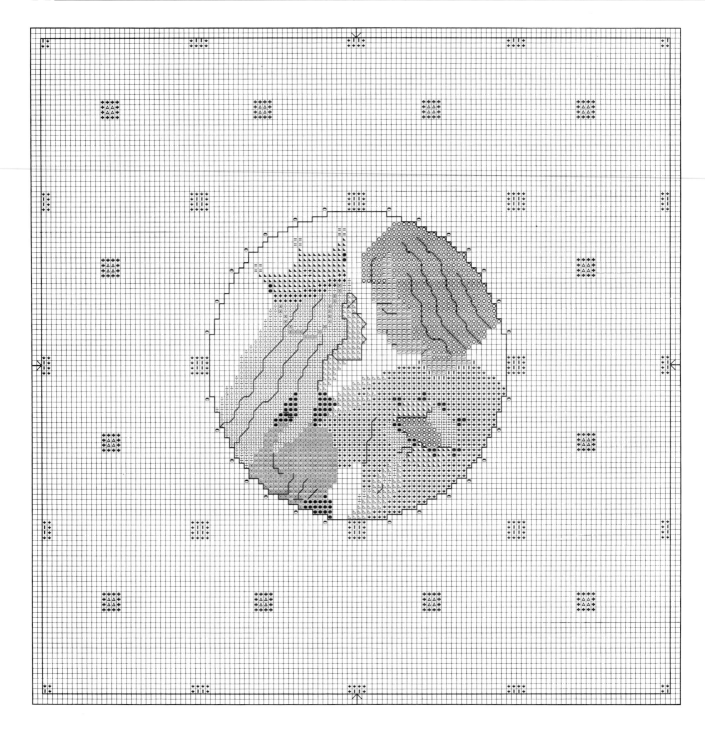

THE SWINEHERD ▲

= white

☘ white seed pearls

○ 834 pale gold (bks 680)

÷ 744 yellow (bks 680)

◆ 680 gold (princess' eyebrows)

◣ 725 deep yellow (bks hair line next to princess' face)

S 3779 flesh (bks 680)

◺ 963 pale pink (bks 605; bks princess' eye 959)

✲ 605 sugar pink

⊡ 3706 peach pink (bks 603)

● 603 deep pink

△ 3609 dull pink

↓ 959 veridian green (bks 3364)

I 3364 green (bks circle outline and the square outlining the design)

BEAUTY AND THE BEAST ▼

- □   white
- ÷   727 pale yellow (bks on shawl and dress cuff)
- ◺   3046 pale gold (bks on dress)
- ◣   783 yellow
- ↑   948 flesh (bks 224)
- | 3713 pale pink
- ✳   224 dusky pink
- △   352 pink
- ●   3075 red (bks on snout; bks 731)
- ◆   680 ginger (bks around feather)
- =   747 pale blue
- ⌣   3053 sage green
- ⊡   731 dark olive
- ↙   3051 very dark olive
- ○   3045 light brown (bks 731)

Snowflakes

This charming yet easy-to-make table runner, embroidered in a single colour and in a relatively large stitch, features a series of snowflakes. The edges are hemstitched in a matching colour and simply fringed. A runner as delightful as this can be used throughout the Christmas period and then put away, to be brought out again in successive years to add to the festive atmosphere.

SNOWFLAKES

YOU WILL NEED

For a Table runner measuring 65cm × 46cm (25½in × 18in):

65cm × 46cm (25½in × 18in) of cream huckaback, 10 threads (blocks) to 2.5cm (1in); an alternative fabric such as Zweigart's Tula can be used
3 skeins of red 326 DMC stranded embroidery cotton and 1 skein of ecru for the hemstitching
No18 tapestry needle

•

To fringe the edges, first press the fabric and trim the edges along the straight grain. Using two strands of ecru thread in the needle, hemstitch around the edges, as shown, placing the stitching seven blocks in from the raw edge. Make each hem stitch two blocks across by one block deep. Leave the fringing until the embroidery is finished.

THE EMBROIDERY

Baste the centre of the fabric both ways and then baste a central rectangle, as shown on the chart, to give the positioning lines for the four smaller motifs and spots. The rectangle should measure 140 stitches (blocks) across by 80 stitches deep.

Referring to the positioning diagram and chart, complete the cross stitching, using three strands of thread in the needle throughout. Work each motif with the fabric stretched in a hoop, see page 4. Remove the basting threads and steam press the runner on the wrong side, if needed. Remove the fringing threads.

FULL-LENGTH TABLE RUNNER

For a full-length table runner, first measure the length of your table. If you would prefer it to over-hang at the sides, add an extra 20cm (8in) at each end. Decide on an appropriate width, not usually more than half the width of your table, and cut out the fabric. Baste the positioning lines and hemstitch the edges, following the instructions above.

Similarly, embroider the motifs beginning in the centre of the runner. Repeat further snowflakes, in pattern sequence, to fill the two sides, placing a large snowflake next to the two smaller ones, and so on.

PLACEMATS AND COASTERS

Instead of a table runner, you may wish to make individual placemats and/or coasters.

For a placemat, measuring about 26cm × 36cm (10in × 14in), embroider a large snowflake in the centre, and for a coaster, measuring about 12cm (4½in) square, embroider a smaller snowflake in the middle. Hemstitch the edges as for the runner, and fringe to complete.

HEMSTITCH

This stitch is the traditional way of finishing the hems of embroidered napkins and tablecloths. For a fringed hem, remove a single thread at the hem and stitch along the line as shown. When you have finished, remove the weft threads below the hem-stitching, to make the fringe.

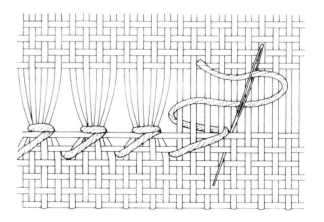

• Bring the needle out on the right side, two threads below the drawn-thread line. Working from left to right, pick up either two or three threads, as shown in the diagram. Bring the needle out again and insert it behind the fabric, to emerge two threads down, ready to make the next stitch. Before reinserting the needle, pull the thread tight, so that the bound threads form a neat group.

SNOWFLAKES ▼

●   326 red

For the positioning lines of the outer motifs and spots,
complete the rectangle, reversing from the centre lines.

TEA-COSY

YOU WILL NEED

For a tea-cosy measuring 37cm × 27cm
(14½in × 10½in):

*90cm × 30cm (36in × 12in) of blue evenweave
Lugana, 26 threads to 2.5 cm (1in)
90cm × 60cm (36in × 24in) of pale blue lawn
for the lining
76cm × 30cm (30in × 12in) of medium-weight
synthetic batting
150cm (60in) of red bias binding, 2.5cm (1in) wide
DMC stranded embroidery cotton in the colours
given in the panel on page 39
No24 tapestry needle
Matching sewing threads
Tracing paper*

•

THE EMBROIDERY

Cut the evenweave fabric in half to give two pieces,
each measuring 45cm × 30cm (18in × 12in). With
the edges of one section prepared and stretched
in a hoop, baste the positioning lines for the
embroidery, as shown on the chart.

Complete the embroidery, using two strands of
thread throughout, except for the outlines around
both faces and hands, where a single thread is
used. Steam press the finished embroidery on the
wrong side.

MAKING UP THE TEA-COSY

To make the paper pattern for the cosy, first enlarge
the graph pattern given opposite on tracing paper
(see page 6), and cut out. Seam allowances of
12mm (½in) all around are included.

Place the pattern on the evenweave fabric with
straight grain and centre lines matching, and cut
out. In the same way, cut out the lining and the
batting as instructed.

To facilitate laundering, the outer cover of the
cosy is detachable from the lining and is simply
bound around the edges with bias binding.

For the loop, cut 8cm (3in) of contrast bias binding and machine stitch the long edges together.

Fold in half to form a loop. Baste to the centre top
of the front section, laying it on the right side of
the fabric, raw edges placed just inside the seam
allowance.

With right sides outside, place both sections of
the cosy together and baste around the curved edge.
Pin and baste the double-folded bias binding
around the curved edge and machine stitch, using
matching sewing thread. Trim the binding level
with the lower edge. Bind the lower edge in the
same way, overlapping the cut ends by 12mm
(½in). Cut the end with the grain of the bias and
fold under 6mm (¼in) to neaten. Remove all
basting stitches and press the finished cover.

THE LINING

Place the four lining sections in two pairs, each
with right sides together, and baste and stitch the
bottom edges, taking 12mm (½in) seams. Press the
seams and turn each section right side out.

Cut 12mm (½in) from the bottom edge of each
batting section, and pin a batting section into each
lining pocket. Baste along the curved seamline,
then place the two lining sections together and
machine zzigzag along the curved seam. Trim the
excess fabric, close to the stitching, and slip the
lining inside the cover to complete the tea-cosy.

TEA COSY

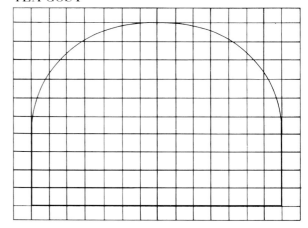

1 SQUARE = 2.5cm (1in)
Cut two from evenweave
Cut two from batting
Cut four from lining

Tea-Cosy

Embroidered in bright, cheery
colours, this large, padded cosy will
keep your tea steaming hot right to
the last cup.

If you prefer to make a cosy for a
coffee pot, it would be an easy matter
to make the sides narrower and
continue the simple, cloudy outlines
of the tree upward to fill the required
space. It might also be a good idea to
add a few more leaves and more depth
to the bottom of the design, to keep
the proportions correct.

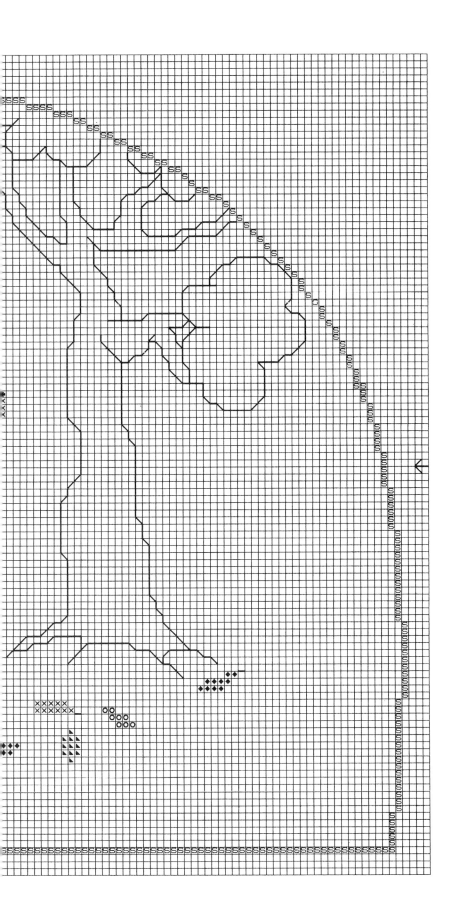

◀ HANSEL AND GRETEL

◇　white (bks 799)

✕　743 pale yellow (bks 833)

=　972 yellow

○　833 deep gold (bks on right
　　tree – second to top cluster
　　of leaves; left tree – second
　　to bottom cluster of leaves)

÷　951 flesh (bks 869)

✚　224 pink

I　223 rose pink

◆　976 ginger (bks on right tree –
　　top and bottom clusters of
　　leaves; left tree – second to
　　top and bottom clusters
　　of leaves)

●　900 red (bks on right tree –
　　smallest cluster of leaves;
　　left tree – top cluster
　　of leaves)

S　732 green

◣　733 olive green (bks tree
　　trunks and branches)

⊖　747 pale turquoise

II　597 turquoise (bks 733)

◺　799 blue

↓　3750 dark blue (bks 799)

⊡　3799 very dark blue

△　869 brown
　　(bks bird's eye and legs)

Dressing-Table Tray

This pretty tray, with its delightful
cross-stitch design of Little Red
Riding Hood and the infamous wolf,
would make the perfect accessory
for a young girl's room, or for
a guest room.
Alternatively, the wintery feel of the
picture, with its bare branches and
the smoke curling up from the cottage
chimney, suggest an unusual
Christmas card, that could be
mounted and hung in due course.

RED RIDING HOOD ▲

Ⲏ white (bks 597)	✕ 729 gold	÷ 948 flesh	✱ 347 red (bks 869)	◣ 597 turquoise
◇ 726 yellow	✦ 977 orange	⊡ 223 pink	‖ 747 pale blue	(and bks sm◦
◹ 833 light gold	= 782 deep orange	⏸ 3328 light red	(bks 597)	bks 869)

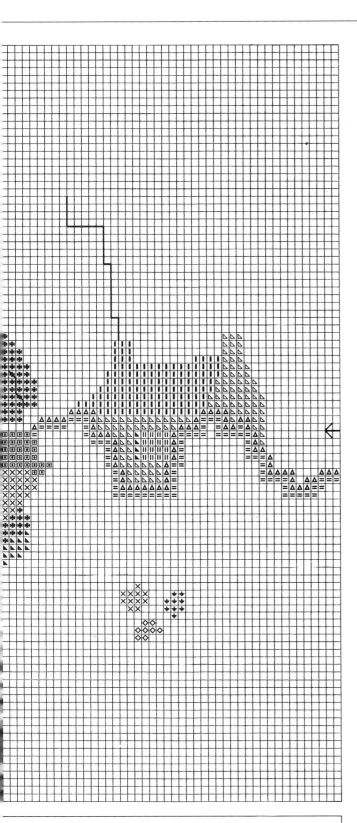

DRESSING-TABLE TRAY

YOU WILL NEED

For a rectangular tray measuring 23cm × 30cm
(9in × 12in) with a 18cm × 25cm (7¼in × 10in)
oval cut out:

*38cm × 30cm (15in × 12in) of grey evenweave
(Aida 718) fabric, 14 threads to 2.5cm (1in)
DMC stranded embroidery cotton in the colours
given in the panel
No24 tapestry needle
Wooden tray (for suppliers, see page 2)*

•

THE EMBROIDERY

Mark the fabric both ways with basting stitches and
prepare the edges before stretching it in a frame.
Following the chart, complete the cross stitching,
using two strands of thread in the needle throughout. Finish by adding the backstitch details on top.

Remove the embroidery from the frame and, if
needed, steam press on the wrong side.

ASSEMBLING THE TRAY

Where the recess is deep enough, as is the case
with this tray, an embroidery can be stretched over
the supplied card, which you may find preferable
to cutting the fabric close to the embroidery.

To centre the card over the embroidery, first mark
the card both ways, using a soft pencil. Place the
embroidery face down with the card on top, basting
and pencil lines matching.

Begin by folding over the fabric at each corner
and securing it with masking tape. Working on one
side and then on the opposite side, fold over the
edges of the fabric on all sides and secure with
pieces of masking tape, leaving the corners at this
stage (see page 7). Check to see that the embroidery is centred; if not, simply release the masking
tape and readjust the position. Neaten the corners
by folding them over to form a mitre and secure
with masking tape.

Insert the mounted embroidery into the tray,
following the manufacturer's instructions.

⊟	471 green (bks 3052)	○	869 brown
⊑	3052 drab green	△	3013 stone
◆	371 light brown (bks 413)	●	413 dark grey

Four Seasons Placemat

This delightful placemat, with its four seasons design, featuring cherries, strawberries, rosehips and cranberries, has a prettily scalloped border, edged with contrast cotton binding.

A single placemat makes a cheerful accessory when eating alone, or it could double as a traycloth. You could also make one for each member of the family, perhaps embroidering just a single motif on each one, placing it at the centre top, to reduce the amount of embroidery involved.

FOUR SEASONS PLACEMAT

YOU WILL NEED

For a Placemat measuring 39cm × 29cm
(15½in × 11½in):

*46cm × 35cm (18in × 14in) of white linen,
26 threads to 2.5cm (1in)
130cm (1½yd) of contrast cotton bias binding,
2.5cm (1in) wide
DMC stranded embroidery cotton in the colours
given in the panel
No26 tapestry needle
Sewing thread to match the contrast binding
20cm × 15cm (8in × 6in) of cardboard for a
template (use a breakfast cereal box or
similar packaging)
Tracing paper*

●

THE EMBROIDERY

Prepare the edges of the fabric and baste the centre both ways. Then, following the measurements given on the chart, baste the central rectangle, which forms the positioning lines for each motif. The completed rectangle should measure 200 threads across by 140 threads down.

With the fabric stretched in a hoop and following the chart and colour keys, complete the embroidery. Use two strands of thread in the needle, and work one cross stitch over two threads throughout.

Steam press on the wrong side. Retain the basting stitches at this stage.

DRAWING THE SCALLOPED EDGE

Using a soft pencil, trace the quarter section of the placemat, as shown on this page. Turn the tracing over; place it on the cardboard, and go over the outline to transfer it to the cardboard. Make sure that the two straight sides meet at an exact right angle. Cut out the template.

Lay the embroidery face down, and place the template over one quarter, matching the straight edges to the central basting stitches. Lightly draw around the scalloped edge. Repeat this for the remaining sections. Carefully cut out the placemat and remove the basting stitches.

BINDING THE EDGE

With right sides and raw edges together, pin and baste the binding around the edge (see page 6), beginning in the corner of one scallop. Where the two ends of the binding meet, overlap by 2cm (¾in), turning the raw, overlapped end under by 6mm (¼in) to neaten it. Using matching sewing thread, machine stitch or backstitch in place.

Bring the binding over the raw edge of the fabric and hem, gently easing it around curves and sewing into the back of the first stitching line to prevent the thread from showing on the right side.

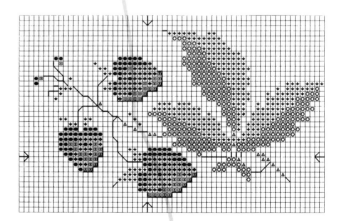

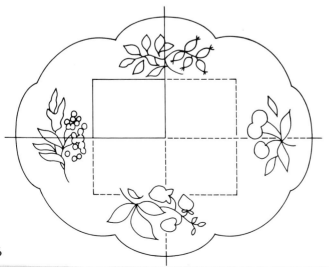

STRAWBERRIES ▲	
⊡ pale pink (bks 335)	● 321 red
✦ 335 strawberry pink, plus outline around light side of strawberry	↓ 470 pale green
	○ 3348 green
	△ 731 olive green (and bks stems)

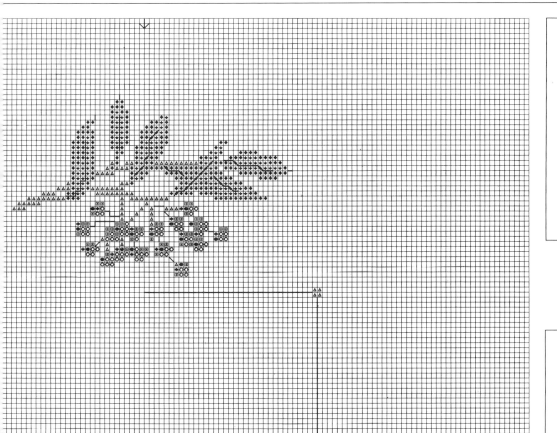

CRANBERRIES ◄

△	744	old gold (and corner spots)
●	718	magenta
○	3752	pale blue
⊡	334	blue
✳	3750	dark blue
◆	564	pale green
↓	959	green (bks 733)

ROSE HIPS ▼

○	676	yellow
●	350	red
△	976	rust
⊡	3766	blue
✳	581	sap green
↓	3012	browny green (and bks hip tips)

To complete the scalloped outline, reverse the template on the centre lines of each quarter section and draw around.

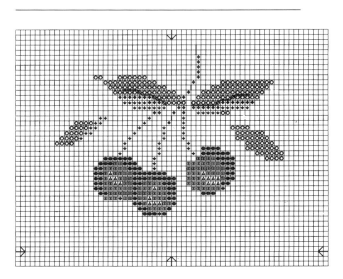

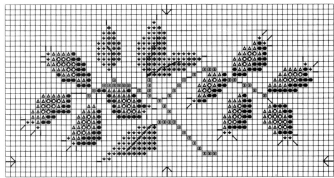

CHERRIES ◄

△	962	pale pink	○	945	pale green (bks 943)
⊡	602	pink	◆	992	sage green
●	600	red	↓	943	veridian green
✳	814	deep red			

ACKNOWLEDGEMENTS

The author would like to offer her grateful thanks to the
following people who helped with the cross stitching of
projects in this book with such skill and enthusiasm:
Gisela Banbury, Clarice Blakey, Caroline Davies,
Christina Eustace, Janet Grey, and to Julie Hasler
for her design on page 12.
Thanks are also due to DMC Creative World Ltd
for providing the black and white charts.

CONVERSION CHART

Not all of these colour conversions are exact matches, and bracketed
numbers are given as close substitutes.

DMC	ANCHOR	COATS	MADEIRA	DMC	ANCHOR	COATS	MADEIRA	DMC	ANCHOR	COATS	MADEIRA
White	2	1001	White	605	(50)	3151	0613	926	(779)	6007	1707
223	895	—	0812	611	898	—	2107	927	(849)	6006	1708
224	893	3241	0813	613	831	—	2109	928	(900)	7225	1709
300	(352)	—	2304	644	830	8501	1907	935	862	—	1505
310	403	8403	Black	646	(858)	—	1812	943	188	—	1203
311	148	—	1006	647	(8581)	8900	1813	945	881	—	2313
315	970	—	0815	676	891	2305	2208	948	(778)	2331	0306
317	(400)	8512	1714	677	(886)	2300	2207	951	(880)	—	2308
320	(216)	6017	1311	680	901	5374	2210	959	186	6185	1113
321	42	3500	0510	712	(387)	5387	2101	962	52	—	0609
322	(978)	7978	1004	718	88	—	0707	963	48	—	0608
326	(59)	3401	0508	722	(323)	2099	0307	972	303	—	0107
334	161	7977	1003	725	(306)	2298	0108	976	(309)	—	2302
335	(42)	3283	0506	727	293	—	0110	989	(256)	6266	1401
350	(11)	3011	0213	729	890	—	2209	992	(187)	6186	1202
351	(10)	3012	0214	731	(281)	—	1613	3012	854	—	1606
352	(9)	3008	0303	732	(281)	—	1612	3045	(888)	—	2103
367	(262)	6018	1312	733	(280)	—	1611	3046	(887)	2410	2206
415	398	8510	1803	734	(279)	—	1610	3051	(846)	—	1508
434	309	5000	2009	739	(366)	5369	2014	3053	(859)	6315	1510
435	(365)	5371	2010	742	303	2303	0114	3072	847	—	1805
452	—	—	1807	743	(297)	2302	0113	3078	292	2292	0102
453	(869)	—	1806	744	(301)	2293	0112	3325	(159)	7976	1002
469	267	—	1503	745	(300)	2296	0111	3345	(268)	6258	1406
470	266	—	1502	747	(158)	—	1104	3348	265	6266	1409
471	(280)	—	1501	754	(6)	2331	0305	3364	(843)	6010	1603
472	253	—	1414	758	868	2337	0403	3609	(85)	—	0710
498	(47)	—	0511	772	(264)	6250	1604	3705	(35)	—	0410
500	879	—	1705	781	308	—	2213	3706	(33)	—	0409
503	876	—	1702	783	307	—	2211	3708	(31)	—	0408
504	213	—	1701	799	(130)	7030	0910	3712	10	—	—
518	162	—	1106	814	(44)	—	0514	3713	(23)	—	—
519	167	—	1105	822	(390)	5387	1908	3731	76	—	—
523	(215)	—	1208	831	(906)	—	2201	3750	(170)	—	—
564	203	—	1208	833	907	—	2114	3752	(159)	—	—
581	(280)	—	1609	834	874	—	2204	3766	167	—	—
597	(168)	—	1110	839	380	—	1913	3772	(379)	—	—
598	(928)	—	1111	842	376	—	1910	3779	4146	—	—
600	65	—	0704	869	(944)	—	2105	3799	(152)	—	—
602	(63)	3063	0702	900	326	—	0208				
603	(62)	3001	0701	924	(851)	6008	1706				